WHAT'S THE BIG DEAL ABOUT

PHILOMEL BOOKS

An imprint of Penguin Random House LLC, New York

First published in picture book format by Philomel Books,
an imprint of Penguin Random House LLC, 2017.
Chapter book first published in the United States of America
by Philomel Books, an imprint of Penguin Random House LLC, 2020.

Text copyright © 2017, 2020 by Ruby Shamir.
Illustrations copyright © 2017, 2020 by Matt Faulkner.

Visit us online at penguinrandomhouse.com

LIBRARY OF CONGRESS CATALOGING-IN-PUBLICATION DATA
Names: Shamir, Ruby, author. | Faulkner, Matt, illustrator.
Title: What's the big deal about first ladies / written by Ruby Shamir ;
illustrated by Matt Faulkner.
Description: New York, NY : Philomel Books, 2020. | Series: What's the big
deal about ... | "Chapter book first published in ... 2020." | Includes
bibliographical references. | Audience: Ages 6–9 | Audience: Grades 2–3
| Summary: "A kid-friendly look at the first ladies of the U.S"—
Provided by publisher.
Identifiers: LCCN 2019032310 | ISBN 9780593114865 (hardcover)
| ISBN 9780593114834 (paperback) | ISBN 9780593114841 (kindle edition)
| ISBN 9780593114858 (epub)
Subjects: LCSH: Presidents' spouses—United States—Juvenile literature. |
Presidents' spouses—United States—Biography—Juvenile literature.
Classification: LCC E176.2 .S53 2020 | DDC 973.09/9 [B]—dc23
LC record available at https://lccn.loc.gov/2019032310

Manufactured in China by
RR Donnelley Asia Printing Solutions Ltd.
HC ISBN 9780593114865 / 10 9 8 7 6 5 4 3 2 1
PB ISBN 9780593114834 / 10 9 8 7 6 5 4 3 2 1

Chapter book edited by Talia Benamy. Original picture book edited by Jill Santopolo.
Design by Jennifer Chung. Text set in Adobe Jenson Pro.

The art was created in three stages: first, thumbnail sketches—many small sketches
created for each illustration emphasizing page design, visual narrative, and light
source; second, intermediate sketches—several sketches created to refine the design
of the book's characters and their environment, details, etc.; and third, the final
art, which was created with watercolor and pencil on sanded Arches
140 lb. cold press paper.

WHAT'S THE BIG DEAL ABOUT

First Ladies

written by **Ruby Shamir**

illustrated by **Matt Faulkner**

PHILOMEL BOOKS

For my mother, Nira Shamir, who taught me
all about women's power. And for Nick,
ever and always a source of my strength.
—R.S.

For Tim and Randy.
Thank you.
And for Kris, always.
—M.F.

WELCOME TO THE WHITE HOUSE

Imagine for a moment that one of your parents became president of the United States. What would your first day in the White House feel like? One "first kid" invited friends over for a massive scavenger hunt. Other first kids ransacked the freezer for ice cream left inside, and some became convinced that the giant mansion was haunted.

One thing is certain: There'd be a lot of changes in store for you and your family. If your dad was elected president, your mom might become the First Lady of the United States, one of the most famous women in the world.

First ladies are a part of the president's team

right from the start. Nancy Reagan stood by President Reagan's side when he took the oath of office and Michelle Obama, the first African American first lady, danced with her husband at inaugural balls celebrating his swearing in.

Everyone knows that being president is a major job, but what about being first lady? What's the big deal about first ladies, anyway?

WHO IS THE
FIRST LADY?

Every president of the United States (so far) has been a man. And almost every first lady has been the president's wife. At the same time, first ladies have also been mothers and grandmothers, sisters and aunts, teachers, lawyers, and even dancers. Some never attended formal schools, while others studied for many, many years. No two first ladies did the job in the same way, but every first lady was a partner to the president and left her mark.

The very first first lady was Martha Washington. After America fought a long revolutionary war to break away from the king of England, George

Washington refused to become king, and his wife, Martha, would not be a queen. He was elected president, and she was called the first lady, a title that has stuck ever since.

The work of first ladies has changed over the years. That's because women in America weren't always allowed to do things that men were. For a long time, women couldn't vote, own land, attend most colleges, or have certain kinds of jobs. That wasn't fair at all, but over time, women fought for those rights—and won! And as women gained more rights, first ladies got much busier.

The first time a first lady did something new, it was a big deal, but after a while, it became part of the job. Julia Grant was the first first lady to issue a special notice to journalists called a "press release." She gave interviews and opened up White House events to curious reporters, something that first ladies do all the time now.

And Carrie Harrison lived at the White House when electric lights were first installed there (and she was scared she'd get zapped by the switches— that's something first ladies don't worry about today!).

Not every president's wife did the job of first lady. Sometimes she was too ill or, in a few cases, the president wasn't married at all. When that happened, daughters, daughters-in-law, aunts, nieces, or sisters took over.

Hi, I'm
Abby
★1★

Hi, I'm
Emily
★2★

Hi, I'm
Molly
★3★

Hi, I'm
Harriet
★4★

1. Jane Pierce's aunt 2. Rachel Jackson's niece
3. Ellen Arthur's sister-in-law 4. James Buchanan's niece
5. Hannah Van Buren's daughter-in-law 6. Letitia
Tyler's daughter-in-law 7. Eliza Johnson's daughter

Hi, I'm Angelica ★5★

Hi, I'm Priscilla ★6★

Hi, I'm Mary ★7★

Hi, I'm Patsy ★8★

Hi, I'm Jane ★9★

Hi, I'm Abby ★10★

Hi, I'm Mary ★11★

Hi, I'm Martha ★12★

Hi, I'm Betty ★13★

8. Martha Jefferson's daughter 9. Anna Harrison's daughter-in-law 10. Abigail Fillmore's daughter 11. Carrie Harrison's daughter 12. Eliza Johnson's daughter 13. Peggy Taylor's daughter

WHAT'S THE
FIRST LADY'S JOB?

First ladies have a lot to do. They give the president advice, meet with people and try to help them, visit foreign lands and leaders, write books, make speeches, and much more. First ladies didn't always do all of those things. But one job that every single first lady has had to do is host guests at the White House. You could say this makes her the "hostess in chief"!

First ladies got this job because a long time ago, women weren't allowed to attend parties at the White House hosted by men unless there was an official hostess present—a woman—to welcome and entertain them. Strange but true!

First ladies are in charge of huge events several times a week for hundreds, sometimes thousands, of people. And sometimes their guests don't get along with one another, so first ladies have to make sure these events are so much fun that enemies put aside their differences.

Sometimes White House entertaining was a family affair. In just six months, Ellen Wilson organized White House weddings for two of her daughters—"I do" times two!

Hosting parties sounds like lots of fun, but it can be lots of work too. Remember your last birthday party? Maybe you and your parents planned a theme, hung decorations, set out the food, baked a cake, prepared goody bags, made sure your guests were having a good time—the to-do list can go on and on.

Every first lady entertained in her own special way. Ida McKinley insisted on hosting events even when she was ill, and often was carried into receptions and laid out on pillows. Julia Tyler threw extravagant parties. At her Grand Finale Ball, she lit up the room with 1,000 candles and played hostess to 3,000 guests! Lucy Hayes, who was first lady at a time when alcoholic drinks were banned at the White House, entertained with lemonade, and later got the nickname "Lemonade Lucy." And dancing wasn't allowed in Sarah Polk's White House.

Dolley Madison was one of America's earliest and most fun-loving first ladies. Her weekly receptions were called "crushes" because so many people filled the White House that they were squeezed together. She served ice cream in special pastry shells that became all the rage. Her favorite flavor? Oyster ice cream!

These parties weren't just about having a good time—they gave the president and first lady a chance to meet people, learn about their problems, and figure out ways to help. Dolley made Americans feel welcome at the White House. And parties like hers helped people across the country get to know the president and his family.

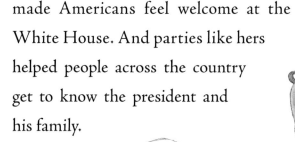

IS IT FUN TO BE
SO FAMOUS?

Sometimes, but not always. If your mom really did become the first lady, photographers would suddenly show up whenever she came to your soccer practice and would follow you both around trying to take your picture everywhere you went. And if you or your mom did something embarrassing by accident—like trip and fall on the White House steps—everyone in the country would know about it.

Some first ladies really hated all the attention. Louisa Adams called the White House a "dull and stately prison." Edith Roosevelt made sure that new White House renovations separated the private living spaces from the offices so she didn't have to worry about strangers getting in the way of her six kids (and loads of pets).

Other first ladies stayed away from the White House for a while. Bess Truman kept a more normal routine by spending time at home in Missouri instead of at the White House, but her husband

wrote to her often, relied on her advice, and called her "the boss." When Melania Trump became first lady, she remained in New York City for the first six months so that her son wouldn't have to switch schools in the middle of the school year.

It was hard even for those who were more comfortable in the spotlight. Frances Cleveland,

the first first lady ever to give birth at the White House, was so popular that her face appeared on everything from playing cards to sewing kits.

Frances Cleveland and her children got a lot of attention from the public. One of her daughters supposedly had a candy bar—Baby Ruth—named after her! That's not all. Once, a stranger visiting the White House tried to clip off a chunk of baby Ruth's hair as a keepsake. Yikes!

BUT IT'S COOL TO LIVE IN THE WHITE HOUSE, RIGHT?

With its own bowling alley, movie theater, swimming pool, and library, living at the White House can be pretty terrific. First kids found lots more ways to have fun there too. One president's son rode his bike down the stairs right into the fancy East Room. Some played hide-and-seek in the grand official state rooms, and others hosted slumber parties on the huge Lincoln Bed.

But back in the early days, White House living wasn't quite as great. Abigail Adams was the first first lady to live at the White House. She got there before construction was finished, so she hung her laundry to dry in what became the East Room! And Elizabeth Monroe didn't care about making the White House fun. She made it look like an elegant European palace instead.

Sometimes, living in the White House can be dangerous. During the War of 1812, the British set fire to the

White House. When Dolley Madison saw what was happening, she quickly threw important presidential papers and a famous painting of George Washington into her wagon and escaped in the nick of time. To this day, you can see the burn marks on some of the mansion's entryway stones.

There were many times over the years when things started to fall apart at the White House and it was up to first ladies to fix them, always making sure to keep the "people's house" beautiful, welcoming, and true to its historic roots.

Mamie Eisenhower started a trend when she decorated her private rooms in all pink—pink pillows, pink bath towels, pink furniture, pink flowers, a pink hamper, and even a pink garbage can—making it the most popular color of the 1950s. And Jackie Kennedy helped turn the White House into a living museum of the presidency. She loved finding and displaying hidden treasures that told the story of America's past. Movers were shocked one day to find Jackie Kennedy—only ever seen in the most elegant clothes—wearing jeans and a sweater to haul and unpack heavy antiques from the back of a truck!

Fun fact: As wife of the first vice president, Abigail Adams was the first-ever second lady. But there's more to her story. As the wife of the second president, she was also the second first lady. Now there's a twist!

WHAT HAVE THE FIRST LADIES DONE BEFORE BECOMING FIRST LADIES?

First ladies have worked in law, dance, and photography, and many first ladies were teachers. Some of them even taught the presidents they were married to!

Abigail Fillmore was the first first lady to work for pay before she was married. She was a teacher, and one of her students, Millard Fillmore, became her husband—and president of the United States. She loved reading so much that she helped start the first public library in her town. As first lady, she helped establish the White House library and kept it stocked with books.

Eliza Johnson taught her husband, the future

president Andrew Johnson, to read and write better. When Florence Harding was a young mother, she earned money by teaching piano lessons. And Laura Bush was a teacher and a librarian before she met her husband. When she was first lady, she hosted the first National Book Festival in Washington, DC. Once, she even got to read a book on TV with Big Bird and Elmo!

Grace Coolidge was famous for having a pet raccoon named Rebecca, but she was also a teacher of deaf children and encouraged President Coolidge to pay attention to people with disabilities.

Barbara Bush wasn't a teacher herself, but she wrote a book starring her dog, Millie, and gave the money she made from it to programs that teach reading.

WHAT DO FIRST LADIES DO OUTSIDE THE WHITE HOUSE?

Beyond the White House grounds, many first ladies worked hard to make our nation's capital, our country, and the world a safer, healthier, and happier place. Sometimes they comforted folks they met who had been hurt, and sometimes they inspired people to help others.

Several first ladies were especially helpful during wartime. During the Revolutionary War, Martha Washington stayed in field encampments, nursed injured soldiers, and organized women to roll bandages for the soldiers' wounds. When she became first lady, Martha met with veterans, or former soldiers, and their families to let them know how much she and President Washington valued their service to the new nation.

World War I was raging while Edith Wilson was first lady. She supported the war effort by decoding secret messages from countries that were America's partners, or allies. She also kept a flock of sheep on the South Lawn—they helped keep the grass trimmed and their wool raised money for the Red Cross, an organization that helps people all over the world who suffer in emergencies, wars, and natural disasters.

Eleanor Roosevelt was first lady during the Great Depression, when millions of Americans lost their jobs and many families went hungry or lost their homes. She did lots of new things no first lady had ever done before, all while trying to help as many people as she could. Eleanor traveled around the country learning about the troubles facing the poor, sick, and powerless, and during World War II she even trudged through jungles and field hospitals visiting 400,000 American soldiers fighting all over the world!

Some first ladies knew that plants could make the air cleaner and neighborhoods more beautiful. Nellie Taft helped bring thousands of cherry blossom trees to Washington, DC. Every spring they shower the area with delicate pink petals. Lady Bird Johnson made sure that trees, shrubs, and flowers were planted all over Washington, DC—and all over the country. She even started a children's garden on the White House grounds.

During a historic trip to China, Pat Nixon inspired China's leaders to donate two panda bears, who made their way to the National Zoo in Washington, DC. When they arrived, she joked about the outbreak of "Panda-monium!"

WHERE IN THE WORLD HAVE FIRST LADIES TRAVELED?

First ladies have traveled to every continent on the planet (except for Antarctica) to represent America. And everywhere they went, they met all sorts of people—kings and kids; artists and athletes; patients and pioneers. They've visited sparkling palaces, holy temples, makeshift schools, and hospital tents. And they've ridden on everything, including ships, military planes, helicopters, trains, and the backs of elephants and camels— Jackie Kennedy famously rode an elephant in India and Laura Bush rode a camel in Jordan. Eleanor Roosevelt even piloted a plane once!

Many first ladies used their travels to try to help people across the globe. On one trip, Pat Nixon shook hands with a patient stricken with a dangerous disease called leprosy, showing the world not to be afraid of people with the illness and to treat them with kindness.

Barbara Bush and her husband ate two Thanksgiving dinners in one day with American troops stationed in Saudi Arabia during the Gulf War. That's a lot of turkey and stuffing!

Rosalynn Carter visited many countries, including Thailand, where she met people who had run away from violence and war in nearby Cambodia. She encouraged world leaders to help the suffering refugees. Nancy Reagan visited with Pope John Paul II in his private study to talk about helping people who were addicted to drugs.

How Else Have First Ladies Tried to Help People?

Staying healthy was a big deal to a lot of first ladies. Early first ladies lived at a time when common infections or colds could turn deadly, so many first ladies were busy caring for sick loved ones or even trying to stay healthy themselves. Today's first ladies encourage people beyond their own families to get healthy in new ways.

Sometimes, this means speaking publicly about illnesses that people are shy to discuss. When Betty Ford was struck with breast cancer, she bravely talked about it at a time when most people avoided discussing it, and she inspired women to get examined by doctors. Rosalynn Carter got Congress to make a law helping people with mental illnesses. For a long time people felt embarrassed to talk about mental illness, but she tried to change that.

Many first ladies worked around the world to help people who were suffering. Laura Bush helped millions of people in Africa get lifesaving AIDS medicine. This helped hundreds of thousands of babies to be born free of the disease.

All of these first ladies and others used their power to teach kids and grown-ups about healthy lifestyles.

Just say no

Some first ladies focused on children's health. Nancy Reagan urged kids to "Just Say No" to drugs that would harm their bodies. Michelle Obama encouraged kids to get active and stay healthy, and she pushed for all neighborhoods to have safe, fun places for kids to play. She even invited kids to Washington, DC, to plant and harvest veggies in the White House kitchen garden.

HAVE FIRST LADIES SPOKEN OUT FOR WOMEN'S RIGHTS?

Definitely. As far back as Abigail Adams, who advised her husband to "Remember the Ladies," there were first ladies who believed that women and girls should have the same rights and opportunities as men and boys—like the right to vote, own property, speak their minds, study any subject they want in school, and work at any job they're qualified for.

Even first ladies from different backgrounds who held different political beliefs felt that women should be able to vote and that laws for men should be the same as laws for women. In the 1920 presidential election, Florence Harding became the first first lady to vote for her husband, because before then—for nearly the first 150 years of American history—women in America didn't have the right to vote!

One of the most famous trailblazers for women and girls around the world is Hillary Clinton. Even though some people tried to stop her, when she was first lady she traveled all the way to China to give a speech declaring that "human rights are women's rights, and women's rights are human rights, once and for all." She has worked hard to make sure that girls everywhere will one day be able to go to school and have the same rights as boys.

Seems obvious, right? But some women and girls in other parts of the world still don't enjoy the rights we have as Americans, and she was standing up for them.

1. Lady Bird Johnson 2. Betty Ford 3. Rosalynn Carter 4. Lou Hoover 5. Pat Nixon 6. Julia Grant 7. Florence Harding 8. Barbara Bush 9. Jackie Kennedy 10. Eleanor Roosevelt 11. Ellen Wilson 12. Carrie Harrison 13. Hillary Rodham Clinton 14. Nellie Taft 15. Laura Bush 16. Michelle Obama 17. Abigail Adams 18. Frances Cleveland 19. Lucretia Garfield

Lots of first ladies were trailblazers in their times, and they helped create opportunities for the next generations of young women and girls. Carrie Harrison was one first lady who did just that: she helped make sure that Johns Hopkins School of Medicine accepted women as students so that they could become doctors. Lou Hoover was the first woman to graduate from Stanford University with a geology degree. She encouraged young girls to pursue their dreams, which was why she was a big booster of the Girl Scouts—and served as its president.

HOW ELSE HAVE FIRST LADIES STOOD UP FOR PEOPLE?

Many first ladies have used their influence and power to help people overcome discrimination, or unequal treatment, based on the color of their skin, their religion, the kinds of illnesses or disabilities they might have, whom they love, or where they are from.

African Americans were forced to be slaves a long time ago in America. Sadly, many of our presidents and first ladies enslaved people. But Mary Todd Lincoln hated slavery and, in partnership with her husband, President Lincoln, she fought to end it. To show her fellow Americans that the color of a person's skin shouldn't matter, Mary was the first first lady to welcome African Americans to the White House as guests.

After slavery was outlawed, African Americans still weren't always treated equally, and a number of first ladies spoke out against racism and all forms of discrimination.

When Marian Anderson, a famous classical singer, was banned from a concert hall because she was African American, Eleanor Roosevelt made sure she got to sing at a much bigger venue—the Lincoln Memorial! Lady Bird Johnson traveled around the country and spoke out in support of an important law President Johnson signed called the Civil Rights Act, which was meant to ensure that all Americans would be treated equally under the law. Barbara Bush spoke against discrimination of people with an illness called AIDS, and she encouraged President Bush to help them.

Eleanor Roosevelt felt that all people should be treated with dignity. After she left the White House, President Truman chose her to represent America at the United Nations, an organization of most of the countries in the world, where she stood up for human rights, supporting freedom, justice, and fairness for all people.

WHAT DO FIRST LADIES DO AFTER THEY LEAVE THE WHITE HOUSE?

Like Eleanor, many first ladies continued to make a difference after leaving the White House. Betty Ford opened up a health center to help people recover from drug and alcohol addiction, and Jackie Kennedy led efforts to preserve historic landmarks like beautiful old buildings and train stations.

Among the many firsts that first ladies accomplished, only one was voted into office herself. Hillary Clinton was the first first lady to be elected to the US Senate, and her husband, Bill Clinton, campaigned for her too. But even more extraordinary, she's the first first lady to ever run for president and come close to being elected the first woman president. We're not there yet, but there's no doubt that one day we will have a woman president, and we might even have the first first gentleman! When that happens, what do you think the job of the first gentleman should be?

THE PRESIDENTS
AND FIRST LADIES OF
THE UNITED STATES
OF AMERICA

President	Presidential Term	First Lady
George Washington	1789–1797	Martha Washington
John Adams	1797–1801	Abigail Adams
Thomas Jefferson	1801–1809	Martha Jefferson (never served)
James Madison	1809–1817	Dolley Madison
James Monroe	1817–1825	Elizabeth Monroe
John Quincy Adams	1825–1829	Louisa Adams
Andrew Jackson	1829–1837	Rachel Jackson (never served)
Martin Van Buren	1837–1841	Hannah Van Buren (never served)
William Henry Harrison	1841	Anna Harrison
John Tyler	1841–1845	Letitia Tyler (1841–1842)
		Julia Tyler (1844–1845)
James K. Polk	1845–1849	Sarah Polk
Zachary Taylor	1849–1850	Margaret "Peggy" Taylor
Millard Fillmore	1850–1853	Abigail Fillmore
Franklin Pierce	1853–1857	Jane Pierce
James Buchanan	1857–1861	Harriet Lane
Abraham Lincoln	1861–1865	Mary Todd Lincoln
Andrew Johnson	1965–1869	Eliza Johnson
Ulysses S. Grant	1869–1877	Julia Grant
Rutherford B. Hayes	1877–1881	Lucy Hayes

President	Presidential Term	First Lady
James A. Garfield	1881	Lucretia Garfield
Chester A. Arthur	1881–1885	Ellen Arthur (never served)
Grover Cleveland	1885–1889	Frances Cleveland
Benjamin Harrison	1889–1893	Caroline "Carrie" Harrison
Grover Cleveland	1893–1897	Frances Cleveland
William McKinley	1897–1901	Ida McKinley
Theodore Roosevelt	1901–1909	Edith Roosevelt
William Howard Taft	1909–1913	Helen "Nellie" Taft
Woodrow Wilson	1913–1921	Ellen Wilson (1913–1914)
		Edith Wilson (1915–1921)
Warren G. Harding	1921–1923	Florence Harding
Calvin Coolidge	1923–1929	Grace Coolidge
Herbert C. Hoover	1929–1933	Lou Hoover
Franklin D. Roosevelt	1933–1945	Eleanor Roosevelt
Harry S. Truman	1945–1953	Elizabeth "Bess" Truman
Dwight D. Eisenhower	1953–1961	Mamie Eisenhower
John F. Kennedy	1961–1963	Jacqueline "Jackie" Kennedy
Lyndon B. Johnson	1963–1969	Claudia Taylor "Lady Bird" Johnson
Richard M. Nixon	1969–1974	Thelma "Pat" Nixon
Gerald R. Ford	1974–1977	Elizabeth "Betty" Ford

President	Presidential Term	First Lady
James E. "Jimmy" Carter	1977–1981	Rosalynn Carter
Ronald Reagan	1981–1989	Nancy Reagan
George H. W. Bush	1989–1993	Barbara Bush
William J. "Bill" Clinton	1993–2001	Hillary Rodham Clinton
George W. Bush	2001–2009	Laura Bush
Barack Obama	2009–2017	Michelle Obama
Donald J. Trump	2017–	Melania Trump

AUTHOR'S NOTE

The story of America's first ladies offers a window into how women lived throughout our nation's history. Of course, first ladies were usually women of great privilege, and as such their narratives don't reflect the full breadth of women's experiences in America or the challenges most women faced as they were constrained by convention or law. But these accounts show how an ideologically diverse group of women used their symbolic status and power to serve our country and improve people's lives. My own experience working at the White House opened my eyes to the enormous sacrifice, courage, patriotism, and commitment first ladies bring to their work.

Note: I did not capitalize "first lady" throughout unless it was used as a title for a specific first lady, because we don't capitalize the word "president" unless it's used as a title for a specific president.

SOURCES

I relied on a wide range of excellent sources for this book, a few of which are terrific resources for young readers.

★ The website of the White House Historical Association has lots of excellent information on first ladies and White House history. Many of the entries on first ladies that I relied on were written by Allida Black.

★ *American First Ladies: Their Lives and Their Legacy*, by Lewis L. Gould

★ *The Smithsonian First Ladies Collection*, by Lisa Kathleen Graddy and Amy Pastan

★ *First Ladies*, a DK Eyewitness Book

★ *First Ladies: The Saga of the Presidents' Wives and Their Power, Volumes I and II*, by Carl Sferrazza Anthony

- ★ *America's First Families,* Carl Sferrazza Anthony
- ★ *Secret Lives of the First Ladies,* by Cormac O'Brien
- ★ The website of the National First Ladies Library
- ★ *Smart About the First Ladies: Smart About History,* written and illustrated by Jon Buller and Susan Schade; Dana Regan; Sally Warner; Jill Weber

MILLIE

Don't miss the other fun and fact-filled books in this series!

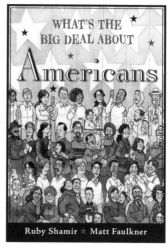